Body Systems

The Skeletal and Muscular Systems

How Can I Stand On My Head?

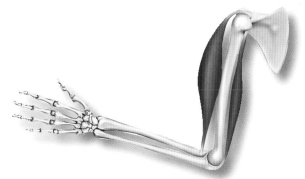

Sue Barraclough

Heinemann Library
Chicago, Illinois

© Heinemann Library 2008
a division of Pearson Inc.
Chicago, Illinois

Customer Service   888-454-2279

Photo research by Hannah Taylor and Maria Joannou
Designed by Debbie Oatley and Steve Mead
Printed and bound in China by South China Printing Company

ISBN 978-1-4329-0868-3

12 11 10 09 08
10 9 8 7 6 5 4 3 2 1

Library of Congress Cataloging-in-Publication Data

Barraclough, Sue.
  The skeletal and muscular systems : how can I stand on my head? / Sue Barraclough.
     p. cm. – (Body systems)
  Includes bibliographical references and index.
  ISBN 978-1-4329-0868-3 (hc) – ISBN 978-1-4329-0874-4 (pb) 1. Musculoskeletal system–Juvenile literature. I. Title.
  QM100.B37 2008
  612.7–dc22

                              2008001160

Acknowledgements
The publishers would like to thank the following for permission to reproduce photographs: ©Alamy p.**28** (Jupiterimages, BananaStock); ©Corbis pp.**20** (Adrees Latif, Reuters), **6** (Bill Schild), **5** (Dimitri Iundt, TempSport), **24** (image100, Russell Glenister), **14** (John and Lisa Merrill), **26** (Newsport, Steve Boyle); ©Getty Images pp.**4** (Digital Vision), **8** (Photonica), **17** (Riser), **11** (Stock4B), **13**, **22**, **25** (Stone); ©Science Photo Library p.**19** (Steve Gschmeissner).

Cover photograph of a child doing a headstand reproduced with permission of ©Alamy (Jupiterimages, BananaStock).

Contents

Some words are shown in bold, **like this**. You can find out what they mean by looking in the glossary.

What Is My Skeleton?

Your skeleton gives your body its shape. It is made of over 200 different bones. Your bones **support** your body. Your bones also **protect** soft parts of your body, such as your heart and lungs.

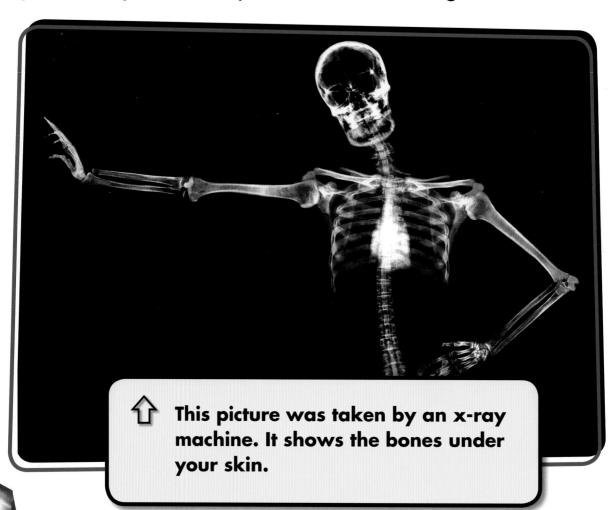

⬆ **This picture was taken by an x-ray machine. It shows the bones under your skin.**

This gymnast shows how her skeleton can bend.

Bones are made of hard **minerals** including **calcium**. A mineral is a substance that your body needs to stay healthy. Calcium helps to make your bones strong. Calcium comes from foods such as milk and cheese.

What Do My Skull and Spine Do?

Your spine is strong to hold up your head. It is also **flexible** to help you move.

Your skull is a group of bones around your **brain**. Your skull **protects** your brain. Your skull is connected to your spine.

Your spine is made of lots of small bones. The bones fit together down your back. These bones allow your spine to bend and twist. Your spine protects soft body parts that connect your brain with the rest of your body.

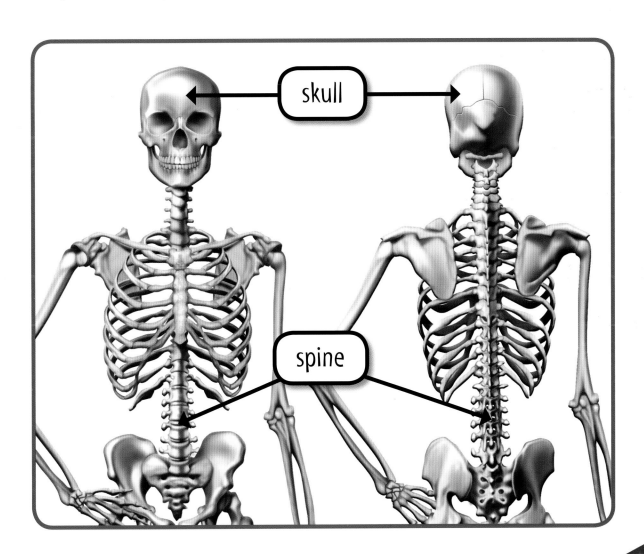

skull

spine

What Are My Ribs?

Your ribs are a group of bones in your chest. They form a hard cage to **protect** soft **organs** such as your heart and lungs. Organs are parts of your body that do special jobs.

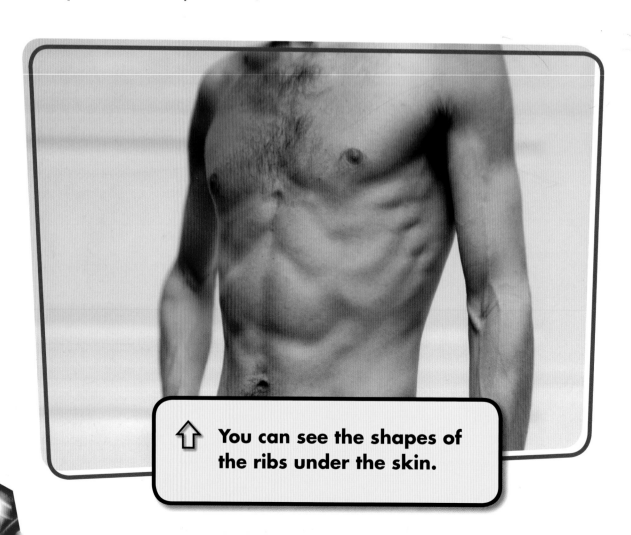

⬆ **You can see the shapes of the ribs under the skin.**

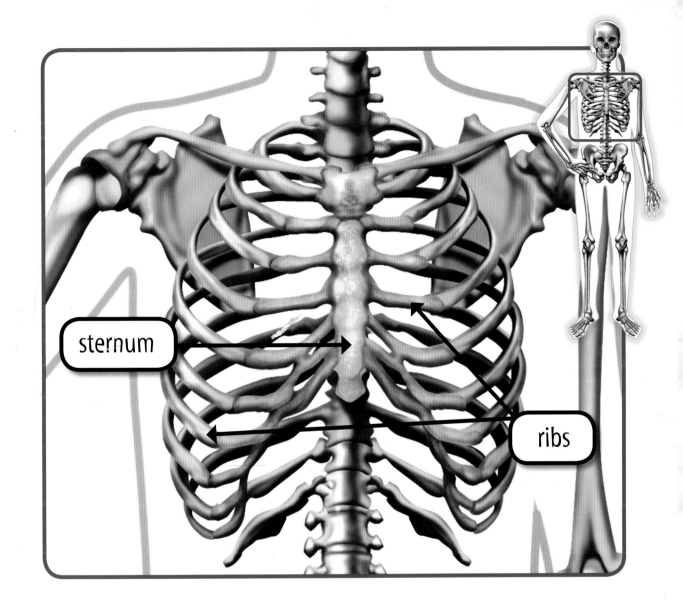

sternum

ribs

Your ribs are connected to your spine at the back. Your ribs curve around to join the long bone in the middle of your chest. This long bone is called the sternum.

What Are My Arms?

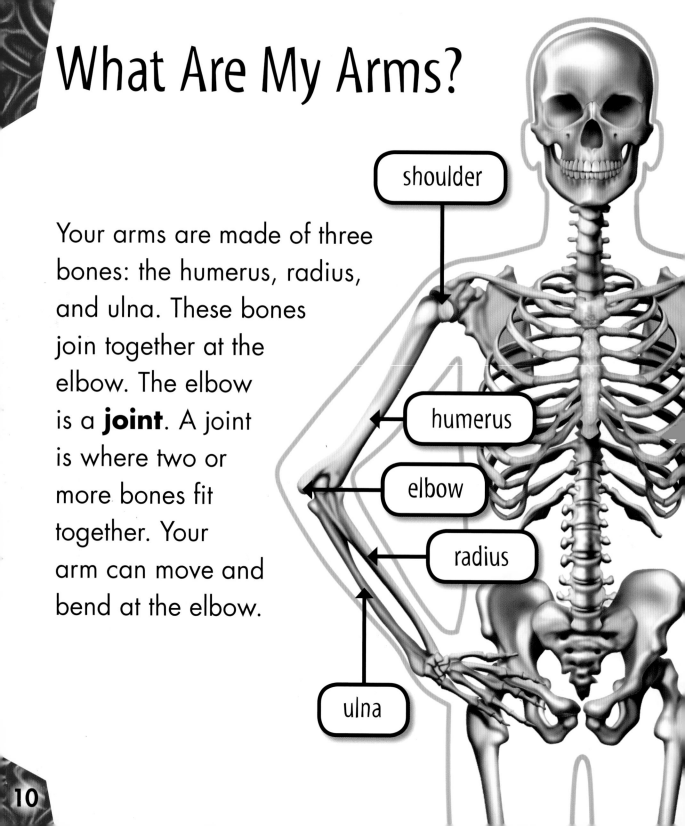

Your arms are made of three bones: the humerus, radius, and ulna. These bones join together at the elbow. The elbow is a **joint**. A joint is where two or more bones fit together. Your arm can move and bend at the elbow.

shoulder

humerus

elbow

radius

ulna

Your shoulder joins your arm to the rest of your body. Your shoulder is a ball and socket joint. This means the round part of one bone (the ball) sits in a round hole in the other bone (the socket). Your arm can move at the shoulder in many different directions.

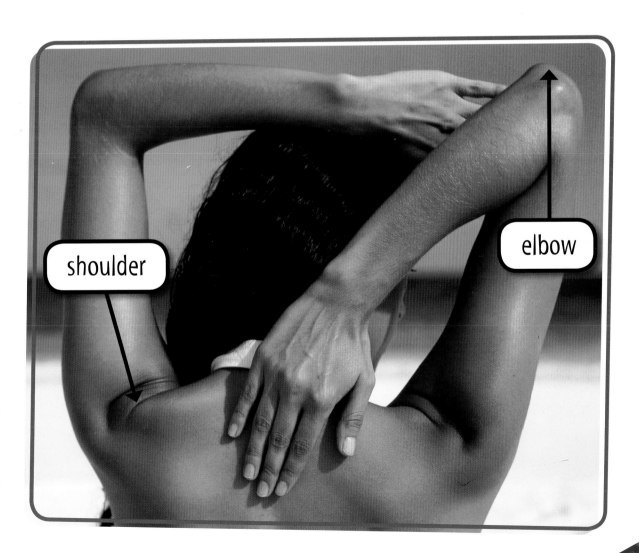

shoulder

elbow

What Can My Hands Do?

Your hands are connected to your arms by wrist **joints**. Your hands are made of lots of small bones. This means they can move and bend really well.

⬇ **You have 27 bones in each hand.**

wrist joint

⬆ **Hands can make the small, careful movements needed to thread a needle.**

Hands can make lots of different movements. You can squeeze your hand hard to hold something tightly. You can move your fingers together to pick something up.

What Are My Legs?

⬆ **Legs bones need to be strong to help you run, jump, and climb.**

Your leg bones are strong to **support** the weight of your body. The bone in the top part of your leg is called the femur. It is the longest bone in your body.

Below the femur you have two more leg bones called the tibia and fibula. These three bones work together at the knee **joint**. Your kneecap **protects** the moving joint. Your legs can move because of your knee and hip joints.

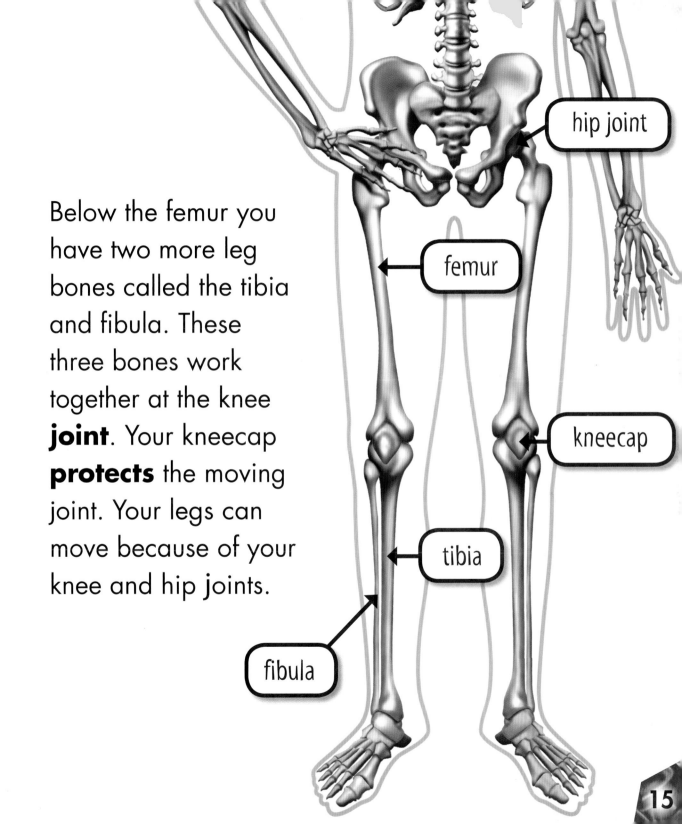

hip joint

femur

kneecap

tibia

fibula

What Can My Feet Do?

Your feet are joined to your legs by the ankle **joint**.
Your feet are made of lots of small bones.

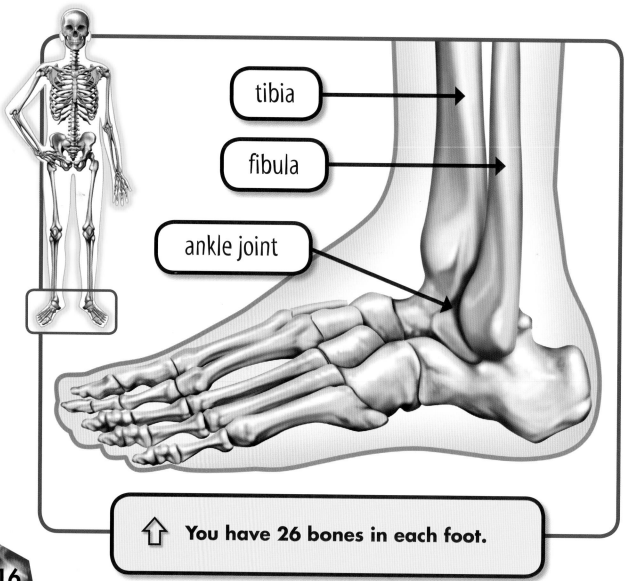

tibia

fibula

ankle joint

⬆ **You have 26 bones in each foot.**

Your feet help you to stand and balance. The small bones in your feet also allow your feet to bend and stretch. This helps you to move around.

What Are Muscles?

These muscles help you to move your face

Muscles are strong body parts which can get longer and shorter. Most muscles help you to move your body. Other types of muscles keep your body's **organs** working.

These muscles help you to move your arm

Most muscles are made of lots of stretchy **fibers**. Fibers are long thin parts like elastic bands. Fibers make your muscles stronger. When a muscle tightens, it **contracts**. Your muscles contract or relax to move different parts of your body.

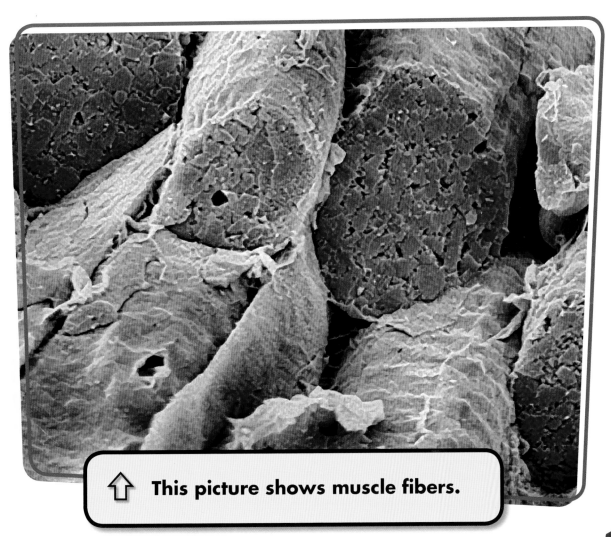

⇧ **This picture shows muscle fibers.**

How Do My Bones and Muscles Work Together?

Your bones need **muscles** to help them to move. Muscles help your bones to twist and bend. They also help you to stretch out your arms to reach things.

Strong parts called **tendons** join your muscles to your bones.

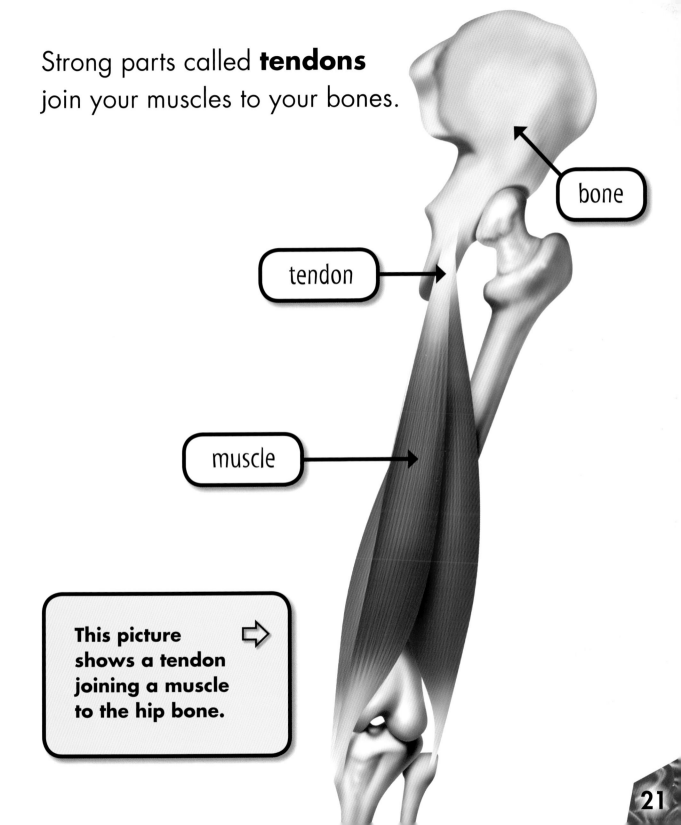

bone

tendon

muscle

This picture shows a tendon joining a muscle to the hip bone.

How Do My Arms Move?

The muscles in your arms work together to make your arms bend.

Two **muscles** in the top part of your arm make your arm bend at the elbow. The muscles are called the biceps and triceps. The biceps pull your arm up, and the triceps pull it back down again.

Muscles work in pairs to move your bones. One muscle pulls the bone one way. Then it relaxes as another muscle pulls the bone the other way.

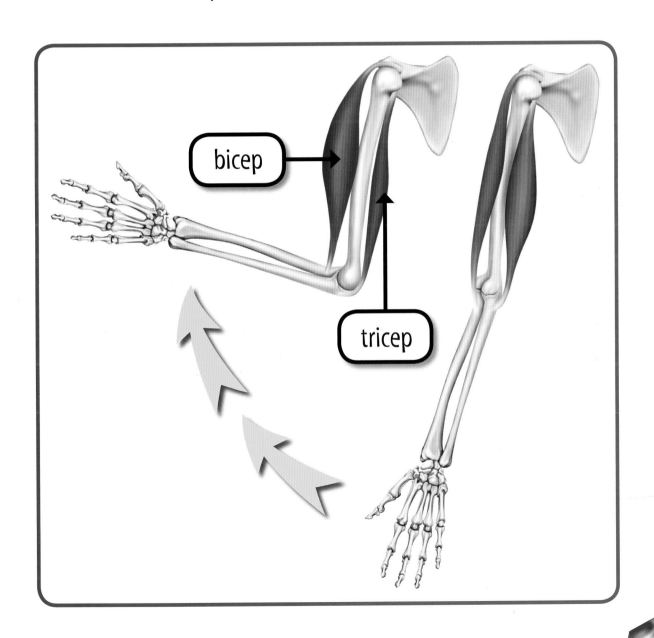

bicep

tricep

What Do My Different Muscles Do?

The strongest **muscle** in your body is the jaw muscle. It is small but it can press your jaw together very hard. Other muscles in your head help you blink your eyes, smile, or nod your head.

This climber uses muscles in his arms, along with muscles in his chest and back to help him climb.

Bigger body muscles work together. They help you do different things such as sit in a chair or climb up a ladder.

The Skeletal and Muscular Systems

Your **muscles** are joined to the bones of your skeleton by **tendons**. Working together, bones and muscles form a strong moving frame for your body.

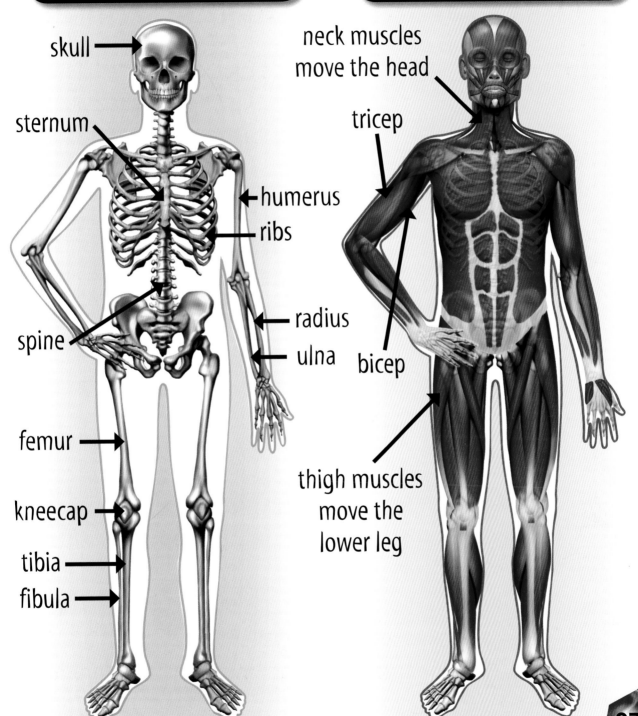

The skeletal system

- skull
- sternum
- humerus
- ribs
- spine
- radius
- ulna
- femur
- kneecap
- tibia
- fibula

The muscular system

- neck muscles move the head
- tricep
- bicep
- thigh muscles move the lower leg

How Can I Stand on My Head?

You use almost every part of your body to stand on your head. You use hundreds of different **muscles** to move the different parts. You bend your spine to lower your head to the ground. You push with your legs to lift them off the ground. Your arms and hands move to help you balance. When you are on your head, all your muscles and bones help you to stay upright.

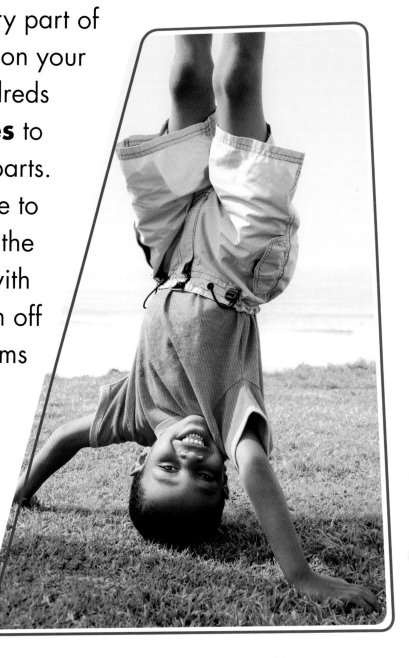

Did you know?

Bones can break but your body can repair them.

Your thickest and strongest **tendon** is in your heel. It is called your achilles tendon. It attaches your foot bones to your leg **muscle**.

Babies have over 300 bones in their bodies. Adults only have 206. As a baby grows many of the bones join together.

The smallest bone in the body is in the ear. It is called the stapes. It is 0.12–0.16 inches (3–4 mm) long. That is about the size of a nail head.

Glossary

brain   organ inside your skull that controls thinking, memory, feelings, and actions

calcium   mineral that makes teeth and bones strong and hard

contract   tighten and become shorter

flexible   able to bend without breaking

fiber   long, thin body part

joint   place in your body where two or more bones join together

mineral   substance that your body needs to stay healthy. Minerals can be found in some foods.

muscle   part of your body which contracts (tightens) and relaxes to move a bone or other part of the body

organ   part of your body that has a certain job to do

protect   keep something safe

support   hold something and stop it from falling

tendon   strong part of the body that joins a muscle to a bone

Find Out More

Books to Read

Ganeri, Anita. *Get a Move On!* London, UK:Evans, 2002.

Royston, Angela. *Get Some Exercise!* Chicago: Heinemann Library, 2003.

Royston, Angela. *Moving.* Chicago: Heinemann Library, 2005.

Websites

http://kidshealth.org/kid/body/bones_SW.html
This website is packed full of information on bones and the skeleton. Find out what bones are made of, how bones grow, how to take care of your bones, and which foods to eat to help keep your bones strong.

http://kidshealth.org/kid/body/muscles_SW.html
Find out about different muscles in your body and what they do.

http://www.biology4kids.com/files/systems_skeletal.html
Find out about why we need a skeleton and how some animals have skeletons outside their bodies.

http://www.harcourtschool.com/activity/skel/skel.html
Put bones in the right places to make a skeleton.

Index